STRIDERS

Stampede!

SCHOLASTIC

Published in the UK by
Scholastic Education, 2024
Scholastic Distribution Centre, Bosworth Avenue,
Tournament Fields, Warwick, CV34 6UQ
Scholastic Ireland, 89E Lagan Road, Dublin
Industrial Estate, Glasnevin, Dublin, D11 HP5F

SCHOLASTIC and associated logos are trademarks
and/or registered trademarks of Scholastic Inc.
www.scholastic.co.uk

1 2 3 4 5 6 7 8 9   4 5 6 7 8 9 0 1 2 3

Printed by Ashford Colour Press

The book is made of materials from well-managed,
FSC®-certified forests and other controlled sources.

A CIP catalogue record for this book is available
from the British Library.

ISBN 978-0702-32728-5

Author
Abbie Rushton

Editorial team
Rachel Morgan, Vicki Yates, Alison Gilbert,
Jennie Clifford

Design team
Dipa Mistry, Andrea Lewis and We Are Grace

Illustrations
Soia De Chiara Manetti/Astound

How to use this book

This book practises these letters and letter sounds:

o (as in 'post')	e (as in 'we')	a–e (as in 'wakes')
i–e (as in 'like')	ie (as in 'thief')	aw (as in 'jaws')

Here are some of the words you will see in the book that use the sounds above:

post   wakes   thief   volcano

This book uses these common tricky words:

all   they   are   their   the   to   you   says   there   pulls some   one

About the series

This is the third book in a series. Cal and Kim are space delivery workers taking packages to alien planets. In the first book they are chased by an angry alien after making a delivery and in the second they crash-land on a creepy planet.

Before reading

- Read the title and look at the cover. Discuss what the book might be about.
- Talk about the characters on page 4 and read their names.
- The story is split into chapters shown by numbers at the top of the page.

During reading

- If necessary, sound out and then blend the sounds to read the word: sh-a-k-i-ng, shaking.
- Pause every so often to talk about the story.

After reading

- Talk about what has been read.

1

Kim and Cal spent all morning delivering post. They are having a doze.

Kim wakes with a start. A thief is stealing their post sack!

"No!" Kim shrieks. "Don't take that."
The thief grins, then sprints off.

Kim shakes Cal awake.

Cal jumps up. They will get that stolen post sack back.

2

Kim and Cal chase the thief
up a steep slope.

The slope begins to shake.
Kim stops. "Cal, I don't think it's safe."

Cal gulps. "It's a volcano. Run!"

They slip and slide down.
The heat is extreme.

They reach the bottom just as
the shaking stops.

"Did you see the thief?" Kim says.
"Over there!" Cal shouts. "We cannot let it escape."

3

Just then, the ground quakes.
"Is it the volcano?" Cal yells.
Kim turns. "No, it's a stampede!"

"Grab a horn. We can get a ride," Kim shouts.
Cal hesitates.
"Be brave, Cal," yells Kim.

Cal shrieks as he pulls himself up.
The beasts thunder off. Kim and Cal cling on.

"Look! The thief!" Kim says.
They dive off and roll in the dust.

Kim and Cal corner the thief.

The thief snaps its jaws.
Kim and Cal back away.

Cal finds some big berries. "We can use these."
He picks one and hurls it.
"Chew on this, thief!"

The thief's jaws get stuck.
Kim grabs the sack. They dash off.

They take the sack back.
Kim yawns. "I'd like a nap."
"No naps!" Cal yawns. "We must protect
this sack."
But then...